Keyword Research for Business:
A How-To Guide

Published by VM Press, Phoenix, Arizona.

ISBN: 1-4565-0297-2
ISBN-13: 9781456502973

Keyword Research for Business: A How-To Guide

What To Look For and How To Find It

James Constable

VERTICAL MEASURES

Cover design or artwork by: David Gould
Edited by: Ardala Evans
Editorial coordination by: Elise Redlin-Cook

2011

TABLE OF CONTENTS

What Is Keyword Research?   1
How People Search—A Look At Search and Keywords   3
Types Of Search Query And Refinement   7
Keyword Research As Market Research   11
Keyword's Influence On Business Strategy   13
Factors To Consider;   15
    Search Volume.   15
    Consumer Intent   17
    Cyclical Timelines   19
    Demographics   20
    Timeliness Of Results   23
    Current Website Strength   24
    Business Goals And Budget   26
Keyword Tools to Use   27
    Word of Warning   27
    Google Adwords' Keyword Tool   29
    Microsoft Advertising Intelligence—Excel Plug-In   30
    Competitor's Keywords   32
    Website Analytics   34
    Keyword Difficulty   36
    MSN Commercial Intent   37
    SERP Results and Current Rankings   38
    Google Instant, Suggest And Related Queries   40
    Google Wonder Wheel   41
    Google Insights For Search And Google Trends   42
    Other Research Tools   44
Building A Keyword Strategy   47
    Choosing Keywords   48
    Content Planning   50
    Measuring Results   51
Conclusion   55
Bibliography / Acknowledgements / Useful Links   57

Foreword

To many, keyword research is a simple process of sitting down and thinking up a list of terms that users might enter into search engines when they are looking to buy the products or services your business offers. For some, this may even include running these terms through an online tool to see the associated search volumes for those terms, and then blindly picking those with the highest volume.

However, for companies looking to get the most out of their SEO or SEM campaigns, keyword research needs to go much further than this to provide you with better information on your potential customers, which will give your business a competitive advantage. Other factors, such as intent, difficulty, business goals and so on, should all be taken into account when making these decisions because ultimately they should lie at the very foundation of your business online.

The aim of this book is to highlight these additional factors that should also to be considered, and show you the tools and resources available to find this information. Armed with this valuable data you can find the most profitable terms in your industry and avoid targeting the same high volume, high competition terms that your competitors are working with.

In addition, the data you discover can help you in other areas to help expand your business offline as well as on. By using keyword research as part of your market research you can discover the growing markets and trends. Understanding what is most important to your customers is key to helping you target them more effectively with all of your marketing campaigns and product development opportunities.

With your target market increasingly moving online and using search engines to find what they want; keyword research is a valuable area to understand in the digital age to find those who are looking for you.

WHAT IS KEYWORD RESEARCH?

Keyword research should lie at the very core not only of your online marketing campaign, but at the heart of your entire business and its marketing strategy. The keywords that we use to search are not limited to our online actions—how we find the businesses and websites that we buy from online—but instead are an indicator of how consumers think, what they want, and how they hunt for, compare, and ultimately buy products or services.

Understanding this information about your customer better than a competitor is, therefore, a competitive advantage in any industry. The medium of search is merely the *how* customers find things online, and not the *why*, which is likely to remain the same offline as well as online. Keyword research can help you understand this "why", and help you better understand who your customers are and what they want. Knowledge in this area can positively impact your offline marketing efforts as well as SEO and PPC, and can lead to superior product development and better business strategy.

In its most simple form, keyword research is the discovery of the search terms that your potential customers are using in search engines, such as Google, Yahoo and Bing, when they are trying to find your business or its products. If your business knows the search queries (also known as keywords) these potential customers are using, and you take the necessary steps to appear highly in the search result pages, then you can increase the traffic to your website and increase your online sales.

Businesses unaware of these keywords will not be targeting them and will not receive this traffic, and their potential customers will instead find their competitors and buy products from them.

Keyword research, on the surface, is just that simple. Discover the search terms people are entering into Google when they want to buy the products that you sell, and then build a SEO or PPC campaign to appear in the search engine results pages (SERPs) so that they can find your business.

However, as you dig down further into this field, things become increasingly complex. I should state at this point that the time and effort you spend on keyword research could be almost as long as you want it to be. There will always be additional data to discover and speculate upon but ultimately you will need to pull the trigger on the terms you believe will send the most value and sales to your business.

Any time that you do spend on keyword research will provide superior results compared to 'going with your gut' and targeting keywords that you *think* your customers are looking for. While the length of this book may be discouraging, it is important that I look at the many different factors to consider and explain the advantages and disadvantages of each keyword research tool available, and explain how to use them together to build a keyword strategy. You do not need to complete all of the steps to be successful; any research into the field will always be superior to guess work that that can possibly set your business up for a failed online marketing campaign before it even gets of the ground.

In addition, the information that you can uncover with keyword research can actually provide you with data that will help you in other areas of your business. You may discover how customers talk about your product, what they look for, similar products that they are looking to buy that you don't currently sell, the demographics of your audience and so on. All of this data has wider reaching implications than just the SERPs and can affect the core of your business, from the products you sell and the market segments you target.

While keyword research is often looked at as a technique used only in Search Engine Marketing, and this will remain the primary focus of this book, the information it uncovers can reveal a more detailed look into your customers' psyche. Companies that invest the necessary time and effort into this area can, therefore, build more successful businesses, both on and offline.

HOW PEOPLE SEARCH—A LOOK AT SEARCH AND KEYWORDS

If you were looking to purchase a new car, find a restaurant for the evening, book a holiday, or buy a new book, it is likely that your first point of call would be in the Internet and your first website a search engine.

As the Internet has grown in use, both in terms of percentage of the population and hours per day spent online, so has the size of the Internet, with more websites, more pages and more information than ever before. As a result, the use of search engines has increased to filter this massive amount of information so that we can quickly find what we are looking for.

With information just a click away, consumers are able to shop around while barely lifting a finger to find the exact product they want at the lowest possible price. This is impeding brand loyalty meaning that successful businesses need to appear in search results for every product they sell, otherwise they won't even factor into the buying decision.

According to comScore, 12 billion searches were performed in September 2010 which equates to 4,500 searches being performed every second of every day. That's a lot of potential business, with customers actively looking to find you and your products to make their purchases.

However, search engines do differ, with different features, different ranking algorithms, and therefore, different results, and it is important to understand the relative importance of each one to reach this worldwide audience. The following table shows the popularity of the five biggest search engines in America, showing just how decisively Google dominates, making it the primary focus for online marketing campaigns:

Search Engine	Market Share (Change from August 2010)
Google	66.1% (Up 0.7% from 65.4%)
Yahoo	16.7% (Up 0.7% from 17.4%)
Bing	11.2% (Up 0.1% from 11.1%)
Ask	3.7% (Up 0.1% from 3.8%)

Table 1—Search Engine Market Share September 2010
Source: http://searchengineland.com/google-up-after-instant-yahoo-down-after-bing-52821

However, these figures vary greatly between countries and cultures, although with Google still dominating in European countries. Certain other countries have their own market leaders, such as Baidu in China, however, for the purposes of this book we shall focus mainly on the three largest search websites which are Google, Yahoo and Bing (the last two of which now share their results). The purpose of keyword research is to therefore find the words and phrases that searchers input into these sites.

With the importance of search engines becoming clear to many businesses for driving website traffic, they are fighting to appear in the results pages for the searches most relevant to their business. But how exactly is this done? This question goes beyond the scope of this book (although the Vertical Measures' book series covers all aspects of this), but in short, it is a case of targeting your website's pages to particular words or phrases that match with those being searched. Once your pages are correctly targeted and match these search queries, your pages will rank higher in searches for these words, and more people will click on those results taking them to your website.

Obviously, if your business sells shoes, you are going to want to rank highly for the term "shoes". However, if you are a small, local business, this is not feasible due to the competitiveness of the term and you would, therefore, want to find and target niche, local or more specific keywords.

In addition, the keywords that this research can identify might not match directly with what you think your business is selling but instead with what your customers want. This helps you to avoid using industry speak that the average man on the street would never use, and never search for. Legally banks have to say that they sell home loans but we search for mortgages, and an industry insider might tell you they sell kitchen electronics but to the rest of us it's a kitchen appliance. Keyword research can help a business find what customers look for even when that isn't what the product is technically called.

Keyword research lies at the heart of any online marketing campaign and needs to be its first area of focus; although it is never too late to correct your efforts. Focusing a campaign targeting the wrong terms can lead to high rankings and even traffic, but with no discernable difference to your bottom line, whereas a focus on the right terms can send your website sales soaring.

Image 1—Google Search Box

TYPES OF SEARCH QUERY AND REFINEMENT

As this book will explain in greater detail later, keywords should not be selected by volume alone but based on a number of other elements such as the intent and what the searcher is actually looking for. There are five basic groups of search queries that different keywords can fall into based on this intent, which are outlined below. Based on the purpose of a website these will have varying levels of importance to your business in sending the right kind of traffic and reaching your online goals.

Navigational

Navigational search queries are used by searchers to bypass typing a website's actual URL, whether it's to save time and effort or because the searcher is unable to remember the exact address. Searches such as "Amazon," "Facebook" or "Vertical Measures" would all fall into this category.

Searchers entering these terms are looking for a specific business, and while it is possible to steal some of a competitor's business by being listed on these pages, it is unlikely that they would click on any result other than the website they were originally looking to find.

Commercial / Transactional

Commercial, or transactional, search queries are purchase orientated and, therefore, revolve around a product name or description. For example, "fast car" would count as a commercial query, as would "John Grisham Novel," "Restaurant in Phoenix," "Brown Shoes" or almost any other term that you could imagine searching for when looking to buy a particular product or service.

The value of these search terms is the highest of the five query types as potential customers are actively looking to buy products, and being listed highly in the results is likely to result in them buying from you, and not your competitors. This is what makes Search Engine Marketing (SEM) so different from traditional 'interruption' marketing, such as TV commercials, as those you reach are actively try-ing to find you to purchase your products.

Informational

Informational searches are focused on finding out a specific piece of infor-mation. The weather on a particular day, the height of the world's tallest man, or whether or not Goodfellas won an Oscar are all considered informational queries.

These searches are less valuable than commercial queries as searchers are not looking directly to buy, however, they can still provide a range of opportunities to a business. Depending on your website, you might be able to build a relation-ship with visitors from these search queries and establish an expert reputation for your business to then turn these visitors into sales at a later date. For example, by providing answers about movies you can build recognition of your website with its target audience—movie lovers—and keep them coming back until they eventually decide to sign up for your weekly newsletter or buy your book.

Pre-Purchase Research

Pre-purchase research is similar to both informational queries and transac-tional queries, although in this case searchers are looking for specific information about products before committing to a purchase. Searchers might be looking for editorial reviews of products that they are unable to find on pure ecommerce web-sites, or for unbiased comparisons to other similar products in the industry.

Ranking higher for these search terms isn't as valuable as ranking for the transactional query itself, but it can still prove very lucrative. Providing the informa-tion that searchers are looking for can reassure them of their purchase decision and result in them purchasing from you, right then and there. In addition, for longer sales cycle products that require a lot of research before making a decision, rank-ing for these research queries can improve brand recognition and trust early in the decision to then capitalize on when they are ready to open their wallet.

Action

The final type of search query is for those who are looking for a specific ac-tion, such as finding an image, watching a video or reading a blog post or PDF file. Along with informational search queries, these are likely to be the least valuable to your business, but still provide a way to get your foot in the door, and your brand in front of your target market.

Providing a 'how to' video can put your business high in the rankings for these search terms, establish your brand as an expert in the field, and can prove valuable later on down the line when customers are looking to buy related products or services from a brand they know and trust.

Using These Search Queries Together

In the real world, however, searches are not usually this clean cut and searchers are usually successful only 70% of the time on their first search. Instead, searchers have search sessions where they get more specific as they build on the information they discovered from a previous query and gain a better understanding of what exactly they are looking for. A typical search session may look more like the following:

Keyword	Purpose	Type
Things to do in Arizona	Research things to do on an upcoming trip.	Informational
Phoenix Attractions	More specific search within the Phoenix area.	Informational
Sightseeing Phoenix	More specific again to sightseeing activities.	Informational
Frommers Phoenix	Navigational search to find authoritative opinion.	Navigational
Phoenix Hot Air Balloon Ride	Search to find companies and potentially make a purchase.	Commercial
Cheapest Phoenix Hot Air Balloon Ride	Further research to find the most affordable company.	Pre-purchase Research
Hot Air Expeditions	Navigational search to the company suggested within previous results.	Navigational

Table 2—Example of a search session

Smart businesses will not only want to rank highly for commercial search queries, but also develop relationships and brand recognition in the early informational search queries where they can reach potential customers before their competitors.

If the searcher in this example could have landed on a page that was written by a hot air balloon company that included a list of activities including balloon rides, then they could have reached their target audience early in the search session. They could then avoid the additional competition that comes with commercial search queries, established themselves as an expert resource and developed a competitive advantage over their competitors fighting for price sensitive searchers.

KEYWORD RESEARCH AS MARKET RESEARCH

The information that you can discover through keyword research does not need to be restricted to use solely in online purchases, but can be used in wider business strategy and can be a key component in market research.

Using the following definition of market research from Princeton.edu:

Marketing research: research that gathers and analyzes information about the moving of good or services from producer to consumer

We can clearly see how keyword research falls into this category by collecting information on the goods and services that consumers are looking for when they search online. If we know that more searches are being performed for "buy movie theatre tickets" compared to one year ago, we can understand that either more people are buying movie tickets across the board or that a greater number of customers are buying their tickets online as opposed to over the phone or at the window. Either way, we just learnt something about either the industry or our customer.

Furthermore, keyword research goes beyond just volume of searches, and we are able to see information related to age, gender and other demographics. Businesses can break down their target audiences into exactly what they are searching for, better understand their needs, and more effectively market the websites and product offerings towards them. For example, keyword research might reveal that men aged 20—40 may search "fast cars" whereas women search for "red cars." Using this information, a business can gain a better understanding of their audience to give them more of the information they require to ultimately make a purchase.

Different keyword research tools (which will be presented in greater detail later) are able to tell you related searches, what visitors searched for prior to the search term where they found you, and what they searched for afterwards. With this information supplementary and complementary products can be discovered, as well as gaps in your product offerings where otherwise loyal customers are being forced to search elsewhere when they can't find what they want on your website.

Not only can you find out all of the above, and more besides, from keyword research and your website analytics, but the data is real world data that is being observed in almost real time. Whereas other market research methodologies rely on small sample sizes, or results being skewed by participants telling researchers what they want to hear, this information is based on populations, not samples, and what actually did happen and what was searched.

For this reason alone, keyword research is a critical activity not only for an SEO campaign, but also for all business operations to better understand their customers, their wants and their needs. With increasing amounts of customers moving online, and more information about them becoming available, a business that ignores this information is going to become uncompetitive offline, as well as online. Conversely, businesses that research and act on this information will be able to perform better across all media by better understanding their customers, and giving them what they are searching for.

KEYWORD'S INFLUENCE ON BUSINESS STRATEGY

With this understanding that more people are spending more time online, and that keyword research's grasp can reach beyond Search Engine Marketing to affect businesses offline, we can take this implication further and see that good keyword research can lie at the heart of business strategy.

As is covered by Vanessa Fox in her book "Marketing in the Age of Google" a business's online strategy *is* their business strategy, and an online strategy should be based around what your customers are looking for. Online and offline do not work in silos and the information that you discover in your keyword research online can also affect the decisions that you make for your offline business. Similarly, the opinions that your customers make about your brand online, will affect their decisions and purchases offline.

If your keyword research shows you that a high number of visitors are searching for complementary or supplementary products that you don't currently sell, then you may wish to seriously consider stocking these products to become a one-stop shop for your customers. Similarly, if your research shows you that there is significant search volume for your products in a different size, shape or color, this might be evidence enough that demand for these variations exists and that product development is necessary to meet your customers demands.

Say, for example, that you are a car dealership and keyword research highlights the fact that men search for "fast cars" and women search for "red cars" when they are trying to find your website. This information should impact the way your car salesmen interact with their clients, the layout of your showroom, and the information displayed on the walls. Salesmen can talk BHP and MPH to the men, and have visual examples of every model in red ready to show the women.

Without knowing how your products are thought of through keyword research, such easy steps may never have been taken and your business may underperform on and offline.Masses of information is available to make better business decisions, it's just up to you to make the best use of it. People searching online are looking for something, and with keyword research you are able to find out exactly what this is and then make it easy for them to find what they need, and buy from you.

This isn't interruption marketing like TV and radio advertising, but is instead people who are looking for products you sell, or at least information about them. Using the data available to you, and tailoring your business and its products accordingly is not only going to lead to higher search rankings, but also better business practices and happier, more loyal customers.

FACTORS TO CONSIDER

As described previously, there are five types of search queries, from informational to transactional, and the value of each can vary from no discernable value, to making a one off sale, to developing a long-term profitable relationship with a target market segment.

The intent behind the searches and the information searchers are looking for is, therefore, an important factor to consider to when selecting the keywords you wish to target. Volume is another factor of great importance, although you should also consider the fact that converting 50% of 100 visitors, is just as good for your bottom line as converting 5% of 1000 visitors.

In addition to this, there are numerous other keyword factors that need to be researched and evaluated in accordance with your business, its brand identity, goals and budgets before selecting the keywords to focus upon for a campaign. The choice of keywords is critical to the success of any SEO campaign, and any online business, and should not be rushed, and instead evaluated from every possible angle.

Below are a number of the most important factors that should be taken into consideration:

Search Volume

The number of times a term is actually searched is likely to remain one of the most important criteria for a business to evaluate their potential keywords. All other variables remaining equal, no business is going to want to rank in the first position in Google for a keyword that is searched 100 times a month when they could maintain that same position for a term searched 1000 times, and potentially receive 10 times as many visits, 10 times as many sales, and, therefore, 10 times as much profit.

However, rarely is the choice this simple, and many tools, specifically Google's AdWords tool, break up their data by three match categories of "Broad", "Exact" and "Phrase". The variation in results between the three of these will vary widely so it is important to understand what each one is saying so that you can accurately interpret the volume data you are looking at:

Broad—This category will always give you the highest search volume as it includes volume data on searches for synonyms, singular and plural forms, and relevant variations of your keywords, as well as searches that contain your keyword along with other words in the query. This information can make your business believe that the volume for certain search queries is higher than it really is, unrealistically inflating your budgeted estimates.

Broad Match Keyword	**Volume data will also include**:
Tennis Shoes	Tennis
	Shoes
	Buy tennis Shoes
	Tennis Shoe Photos
	Running Shoes
	Tennis Sneakers

Table 3—Broad Match Query Types

Phrase—Volumes returned by keyword research tools set to "Phrase" will return the second highest volumes after broad match types, as it includes any search query which include that keyword as well as searches that included other words in the query. Having these volumes for certain categories can remain important in understanding the total value of the market, but will not help you to understand the actual search volume to expect if you rank for these queries.

Phrase Match Keyword	**Volume will include:**
Tennis Shoes	Red tennis Shoes
	Buy tennis Shoes
	Tennis Shoes Reviews

Table 4- Phrase Match Query Types

Exact—Tools set to exact match will provide the most accurate and actionable data from your keyword research as it will show only the number of times that exact search query was made in a search engine. You are able to better compare apples to apples without mistakenly including the volume of queries from other keywords you are not specifically targeting.

Phrase Match Keyword	**Volume will include:**
Tennis Shoes	Tennis Shoes

Table 5—Exact Match Query Types

As a result of these differences, and to make the best decisions for your business and your SEO campaign, we suggest that you set each tool to "Exact" match, or the equivalent, so that you know what the data is telling you.

In addition to these static volume statistics returned by keyword research tools, you will also want to consider the recent trends and changes in the search volume to know if a market is growing or in decline. SEO campaigns are regarded as long-term investments, and it may, therefore, be beneficial to focus on keywords with lower volume today that are increasing in volume, over marginally higher volume today in a market that is in decline. This information is available in a number of tools, as explained in detail later, but the following Google Insights screenshot shows how volume can change over time with market conditions:

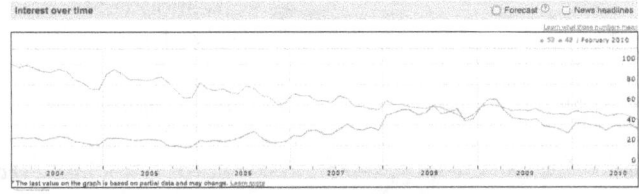

Image 2—Search trends for 'foreclosure', red, and 'new home', blue.

In the above example you can see how the volume of searches for 'new home' has declined steadily since 2004, whereas the searches for "foreclosure" has increased, reaching a peak in early 2009. Businesses can use this data to understand which markets to enter and which search terms offer the most value for the future of the business.

Consumer Intent

As we saw with the differences in types of search query, the intent behind search terms can differ greatly in terms of what a searcher is looking to do when they enter a keyword. Depending on this information, a business targeting certain keywords over others may get greater value from each visit compared to competitors ranking for different terms. For this reason alone, keyword research is not just a matter of choosing the keyword with the highest associated search volume.

For this book, we will mostly assume that business are operating websites to make sales, either through e-commerce or by attracting leads to convert into sales offline. However, businesses operating by different business models, or websites wanting to focus keywords on a secondary purpose, might want to target searches with a non-commercial intent. For example, websites wanting to provide information or customer support will be more interested in pre-purchase and informational queries than those with a transactional intent. Similarly, blogs or affiliate websites might be focused on traffic numbers over targeted traffic for maximum advertising reach.

Another tool we will look at later in this book, Microsoft's adCenter Commercial Intention Tool, aims to quantify this commercial intent with terms more likely to make a purchase than others given a higher score. In the following example, we can clearly see which keyword we would rather rank highly for if we sold cameras:

Search Query	Status
Digital Camera	Commercial—95% Likelihood of Commercial Intent
Digital Pictures	Non-Commercial - 42% Likelihood of Commercial Intent

Table 6—Commercial Intent behind 'Camera' and 'Digital Pictures' searches.

However, as we will see later, selecting keywords is not just a factor of multiplying keyword volume by commercial intent. Yes, "digital cameras" is likely to lead to more sales, but that is not to say that the difficulty to rank for this term wouldn't mean that its return on investment (ROI) is below that of "digital pictures." It is likely to be much easier to create a website showcasing digital pictures to rank in a high position for this term, drive traffic to the website, a percentage of which might want to try it for themselves, and then buy a camera directly. If such as website was run by Canon, they might stand a competitive advantage over Nikon, by getting a superior ROI and targeting customers before they even knew they wanted to buy a camera.

Depending on your business model, its industry, goals and strategy, you may want to target your potential customers earlier or later in the buying cycle, and with varying commercial intent.

For simple, homogenous, low cost purchases, such as socks, customers are unlikely to do any great research before making their purchase and transactional queries for "men's socks" are likely to be critical to business survival.

However, for products with a longer buying cycle that are typically more expensive and need to be compared on a number of levels, a business may be better positioned by targeting their customers earlier in their buying cycle during their pre-purchase search queries. Their website can provide all of the information required to make a decision and gently lead visitors through the sales cycle until they are ready to part with their money.

Cyclical Timelines

The volume data provided by most keyword research tools will provide the information either for the entire year or by giving the average monthly amount over the past 12 months. However, if you are in a cyclical business, such as one that varies over seasons of a year, then you might find this information to be less than useful.

Using the Google AdWords Keyword tool, the following table shows the "Global Monthly Searches" for the keyword "Snowboard", the average for each month, and then shows how this fluctuated across the months of the previous year:

Snowboard	
Global Monthly Searches	110,000
August 2010	6600
July	5400
June	4400
May	5400
April	6600
March	12100
February	22200
January	18100
December	22200
November	14800
October	14800
September	9900

Table 7—Search volume by month for 'snowboard'.

Another tool, Google's Insights for Search, can then show this data visually, not only for the past year, but since 2004 shown in Image 3 in blue. Any business that already operated in this industry will be well aware of this cyclical nature, and for terms like "snowboards" it would certainly appear to be obvious. However, for any business looking to enter a market or develop a new product, this type of information can prove to be very valuable market research, and again help with sales forecasting.

In many other industries, the causes can be much more subtle than the temperature moving towards freezing each wintertime. A lot of B2B businesses may suffer the effects of cyclical trends as budgets for the New Year become available, or belts tighten towards the end of year.

Being aware of these fluctuations through keyword research can help businesses to better plan their resources as well as better understand the market they are potentially entering. In addition, businesses may decide to look for similar markets that work on an opposite cycle so that they can enjoy a steady demand and enjoy year round revenue. In the case of our snowboard company, offering swimming merchandise during their summer months could do this, as shown in red:

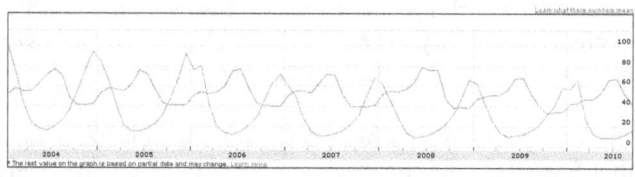

Image 3- Google Insights for Search for 'snowboard', blue, and 'swim', red.

Clearly these are exaggerated instances, and changes can be much more subtle yet still have large consequences on product demand. Any businesses trying to forecast sales based on volume figures from keyword research tools need to bear in mind any cyclical changes and look beyond the given monthly average.

Demographics

The demographic information of who is searching particular terms can help a business to better understand not only which keyword terms they might want to target, but can potentially help them better understand their consumer and who is in fact buying their products offline as well as online.

The actual tools that can tell you this information will be visited later in this book, but first it is important to consider why this information would be a relevant factor in selecting a keyword to target with an SEO or PPC campaign. To help illustrate this point, I will look at a couple of examples involving the terms "engagement rings" and "Ferrari".

If you were an online company that sold engagement rings, it is possible that you would have a marketing strategy in place to target males between 25—35, which you understand to be the age and gender of those who most commonly buy your products, albeit with the help of their fiancés. You might perform some initial keyword research into queries such as "engagement rings" and discover a very high associated search volume and decide that these are the terms you should target with your budget.

It would be a reasonably fair assumption that a large proportion of these searchers where young males who were looking to buy, or research buying, a ring for their fiancé. However, in reality the demographic information behind this keyword search are split as follows;

Gender	Percentages of Searches
Males	28%
Female	72%

Age	Percentage of Searches
<18	8.41%
18-24	49.20%
25-34	29.88%
35-49	9.62%
50+	2.89%

Table 8—MSN Demographic Predictor for 'engagement rings'

Now some of you may have suspected that women would be behind a large amount of the searches for a term that matters to them as much engagement rings might, but for any business the realization that 72% of your visitors are never actually going to buy your product themselves is likely to affect their marketing plan in a big way.

This might not mean that this keyword isn't a good selection for an online diamond ring retailer, in fact depending on the competition to rank well for the term, it probably is good at sending targeted traffic to the website. However, it does affect how a website should market their product, design their website, and budget for online traffic and sales.

As is explained in great detail in his book "Why We Buy," Underhill has discovered great differences in the way men and women shop and make decisions. Men tend to make quick decisions either based on instinct and statistics, in this case maybe carat size, clarity, color and so on, whereas women make their purchase decisions at a much slower speed, based on emotions—how something looks and feels.

A website that is targeted towards men might only need to include one corresponding photo and a chart to compare it against similar items to help them make a decision. Comparatively, a website that is aiming to sell mostly to women might need to include long paragraphs explaining the color, materials and fit, as well as multiple photographs covering every possible angle. A successful engagement ring website would, therefore, have to know their audience and how they should position and structure their business.

In addition, knowing that 72% of your audience isn't actually going to buy your product doesn't mean that they aren't going to be very valuable to a purchase decision, and in the case of engagement rings, the connection is likely to be very strong. Again, this might affect the way a website is designed so that visitors can quickly share a link with their significant other, perhaps via social media buttons or a one click email option that immediately sends all of the purchase information to their future husband. Making this process as easy as possible for the large part of your audience could be a key component to this industry's website design.

Age is the second factor available from demographic keyword research tools, and as the previous screenshot for the term "engagement rings" showed almost 50% of their search volume comes from searchers in the 18—24 range. Given the fact that people now tend to get married later in life once they are able to begin their careers, we might be able to assume that the majority of searchers for this term are not actually looking to buy any time in the near future and are just looking to dream about when that day comes. This would clearly be an important realization into the way a website is used, and perhaps lead to more accurate website goals and forecasting.

On a similar note, searches for the keyword "Ferrari" are split across the following genders and ages:

Gender	Percentage of Searches
Male	68%
Female	32%

Age	Percentages of Searches
<18	16.26%
18-24	29.24%
25-34	26.08%
35-49	21.08%
50+	6.55%

Table 9—MSN Demographic Predictor for 'Ferrari'

While young women search a disproportionate amount for engagement rings, this data shows that young men search for Ferraris, showing where their priorities lay. The fact that many of these men may never actually be able to afford one, at least not until they hit their mid life crisis, doesn't stop a man from looking. A page that wanted to rank highly for this keyword could stock a range of merchandise that this audience can afford, along with images of the cars themselves, to profit from these visitors.

Another example given by Underhill for the offline world relates to this idea that the primary user of a product is not always the one who buys it, is that of children's books. While children, or rather their parents, might be expected to be the ones purchasing most of these books, in reality it most often grandparents looking to spoil their grandkids. However, these grandparents are likely to be more removed from the child, meaning they aren't as familiar with their reading ability and do not know the appropriate books to buy. As a result, Underhill suggests grouping items by age—a characteristic that grandparents are much more likely to know.

While this example doesn't seem to work as well online, perhaps because the older generation is less likely to use the Internet for shopping, the insight it provides remains useful. If a business is able to better understand the audience that is coming to its website from certain keywords, it can better optimize the page for converting visitors into sales by providing more relevant information through superior website design.

Timeliness of Results

Analyzing and identifying potential keywords for a website to target isn't just a case of finding the terms with the highest volumes of searches done by those who are most likely to actually buy your product. In reality it is often a trade off between choosing the best keyword, and doing the best you can with your available resources.

One of the areas for consideration which needs to be included in this decision making process is the timeliness of results required, and its trade off with a keyword's difficulty.

In a perfect market, which the Internet is increasingly representing, you can assume that any profitable market will be entered into by new businesses, and become increasingly competitive until prices are driven down and extraordinary profits are no longer possible. Assuming the online world is at least close to this model, we can say that the best keywords in terms of the number of sales it can generate will be the most competitive. The worst terms that send little traffic and no actual sales, might then be the least competitive to rank well for in search engines, and similarly average terms will have average amounts of competition.

The holy grail of keyword research is finding imperfections in the market, the terms that you think will send a lot of sales that also have lower competition than they should given their profit potential.

The selection of keywords by a business should, therefore, depend not only on the quality of those terms to send sales to a website, but the timeline for expected results, the budget that is available, and the power of the current website to be competitive.

One of the keyword tools that will be explained in the next chapter of this book aims to give a numeric value to the competition for any particular keyword so that a business can compare the potential profits with the cost of ranking highly for that term.

A business that is in need of quick returns from their SEO and any chosen keywords, will perhaps want to stay away from the most competitive and most lucrative keywords until some point in the future when they can afford the associated costs. Instead they would want to target specific niches where they believe they can rank quickly given their budget, yet still make enough sales in the time period to make this activity worthwhile. These sales from these niche keywords might then be enough to keep the business afloat and the money can be reinvested into the more lucrative keywords for future benefit.

The balance of quick results and still ranking for keywords that are going to send some sales is difficult to predict and even experience isn't necessarily going to help as every industry and keyword is unique. However, any business that is selecting its keywords needs to be aware of the trade off between quick results and targeting the keywords with the greatest sales potential.

Current Website Strength

Mixed into the decision regarding the trade off between quick results, competitive keywords and size of budget, is the strength of the business's current website. By "strength" I am not referring to a website's design, or even its current ability to sell products, but instead its strength in the eyes of the search engines.

Search engines rank their listings based on anywhere between 200 and 1000 different attributes, but among the most important of these are backlinks—links from other websites pointing to your domain. Google began on the theory that the best academic papers where the ones most often cited by other academic papers, and turned this theory to websites theorizing that the best sites are those linked to most often. Consider each link as a "vote" for a website as if to say, "I recommend you leave my website by following this link to another useful page."

There are several tools that can estimate the number of links a website has such as Yahoo Site Explorer, and SeoMoz's Open Site Explorer, shown below:

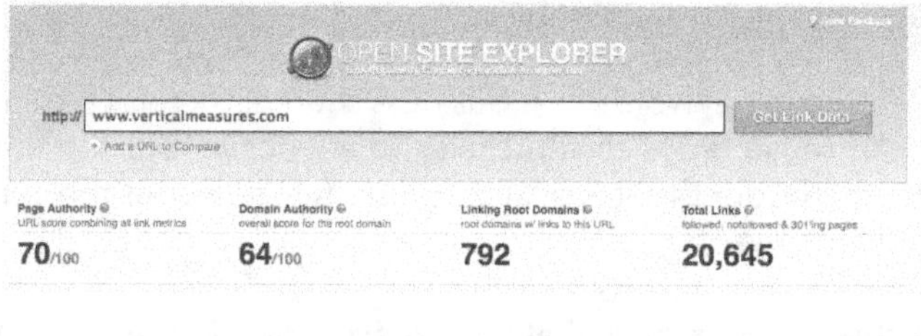

Image 4- SeoMoz Open Site Explorer showing that verticalmeasures.com has over 20,000 backlinks from 800 domains.

Alone, none of these numbers mean a great deal, however, you can put the websites that are ranking highly for potential keywords you might target into this tool and then compare the figures with those for your site. You can then get an idea of how your website compares to your competition and how far away it might be from being able to compete directly for these keywords.

Knowing how strong your website is in comparison to your competition will help you get a better idea of the time, and budget, it might take to build your website up to rank similarly for these terms, which will feed back into the decision making process of choosing best keywords versus getting quick results.

Another approximation of website strength, as perceived by search engines, is PageRank, which is a scoring system given by Google to every webpage on a scale of 0—10. Everyone with the Google Toolbar is privy to this information and it is displayed as a small green bar for every page that user visits. This PageRank can again be compared to competing websites, although given the reduced number of statistics returned (a single number between 0 and 10) this number is less actionable compared to knowing that you need more links, linking domains, or a higher quality of linking website.

You can also use your current rankings in SERP to develop a strong understanding of the strength of your current website and use this information to better understand how long it can take for the rankings you desire for a given keyword.

For the lucky website owner out there, you might discover a new keyword you wish to target and upon searching that term discover you are already low on the first page of results, or high on the second page. If this is the case, without previously targeting this term, it is a reasonably safe assumption that you will be able to rank in the first few positions in a short period of time once you refocus a page to that keyword.

Conversely, if you are not even ranking in the top 100 positions in Google for a low competition term, even this might be hard to break onto the first page in a short period of time, without at least a reasonable budget, simply because of the low strength of your website.

To best identify the keywords you should ultimately select for a business, you need to have a good understanding of its starting point so that you can accurately target the keywords that are going to send the desired traffic in a given time period. As a disproportionate number of visits come from the first few places in the SERPs, you are better placed to target the terms where you can achieve these high rankings, rather than the larger volume terms where you might only be able to advance from page 5 to page 3, and see no significant growth in traffic.

Business Goals and Budget

The final factor in regards to choosing the keywords that you should ultimately target with an SEO, or PPC campaign, has been mentioned throughout this chapter and is the goal of your business and the budget it has to invest in SEO or online marketing.

For the majority of this book, I have assumed that the goal of any website is to make a sale, either on that initial visit when the site is discovered by a prospective customer via a search engine, or at a subsequent visit depending on the length of the sales cycle.

However, for many websites this is not the case, and therefore, makes the Commercial Intent a much smaller factor in keyword selection. Some websites might exist solely for customer service—to provide information to those who have already bought a product. Others might exist for branding, and others, such as blogs and forums, exist solely to unite people of similar interests, and perhaps make a little money from advertising.

Similarly, a business might have goals that mean that they do not want to rank for particular keywords or searches that cater to a particular audience just from a branding standpoint. Smaller businesses might be aware of larger market potential out there that they could rank for, but for the time being they are trying to remain specific to a niche until they are ready to grow with the necessary investment.

The point is that every business, and every industry, is unique and needs to be fully understood to stand the best chance of selecting keywords that are going to send the right kind of traffic to any website. It is because of this fact that no equation or algorithm could ever be used to select keywords that are right for your business. You can only pull relevant data and then make a decision based on your knowledge of the industry and your own intimidate knowledge of the business.

By considering and understanding everything from search volume and consumer intent, to internal factors like goals and budget, you are giving your SEO campaign the best foundation it can have for bringing in new business and improving any website's bottom line. After all, it could be said that the only way to truly evaluate a keyword is through its affect on your company's profits.

KEYWORD TOOLS TO USE

In the previous chapter you hopefully gained an understanding of all of the factors that could be considered when evaluating keywords to make the best possible decision. The next step is to actually collect all of this information so that you can make an informed decision, which is the purpose of this chapter, to introduce you to the right tool for each job.

Some of the tools that will be shown in this chapter have already been mentioned previously in examples when it was appropriate, but on these pages I will explain where to find each tool, when it should be used and what information it is actually displaying. I will also aim to provide some tips and insight for each tool to help you get the most useful information for superior keyword selection.

This book isn't aiming to be a 'how to guide' for each of these tools, so the instructions will be only basic; instead the aim is to give you a better understanding of the information that is being returned and what purpose it can serve in analysis. By using this information in conjunction with the previous chapter you can get a strong idea of which tool relates to each factor and how important its data will be for the website you are currently working with.

Word of Warning

The tools described in this chapter are by no means inclusive of every tool on the market and are just the tools I use most often and would recommend to others. They are not perfect; every tool available has its drawbacks, but I have become comfortable with these tools over time and learnt how to interpret the information that is being returned. Sometimes it is just a case of "better the devil you know."

I would also recommend that you research and try new tools as they become available and do not limit yourselves to those within this book. See which work best for you and your needs, and which you believe give you the best information to give your online marketing campaign the best chance for success.

When using any of these tools and analyzing their data it is also important to think about where each of these sources get their information and how, as well as what they have to benefit from giving you access to this data.

There is no government agency that collects keyword searches, and no unbiased organization that is able to access data from various parties and combine it into one universal picture of online search today. We have no true way to ensure that the information we receive is fair, true or accurate, so I, therefore, suggest that you consider the following factors when looking at any keyword data:

Source—For each of these tools it is worth considering who is providing the information and where they are getting it. Search engines provide many of these tools directly, such as Google and Microsoft (who owns Bing) which means that you are not getting volumes for total online search, but rather each engines portion of that search in the specified region, as shown previously.

Other tools rely on toolbars installed on a user's web browsers, which then attempt to use this sample to approximate for the population. However, toolbars might be more likely to be installed on Internet savvy users than the general population, which can then skew that data you receive.

Incentives—It is also important to consider why these companies are letting you access this information, usually for free, and what they have to gain from it. Search engines make their money from advertisers using their pay per click model to rank highly for their targeted keywords. Tools that are provided by the search engines themselves might be overstating the number of searches for their most expensive keywords, while downplaying the volume for less profitable terms.

The best solution to the problem of having trustworthy data is to always use multiple sources as much as possible to confirm your findings and use common sense as much as possible. If results are using very round numbers you can assume that they are not completely accurate, and if you can't understand why volume for one term is much higher than another, it could simply be a programming bug within the tool—it has been known.

The real key to keyword research is to look for trends and comparisons and not the raw numbers themselves. If multiple sources are able to tell you that one term is searched more than another, it is likely to be the case, and you might then want to target that larger term. You can then use your own website analytic data to get a better idea of what the actual traffic numbers themselves are to learn how close the search volume from these tools were.

The only way to truly get an understanding of accurate data is to collect your own information, either through historical website traffic numbers, or by running a short term PPC campaign. Once you have data from keywords and can see how likely it is to convert into sales on your website, you can get a better idea of how valuable that keyword is to your business and how much budget to allocate to ranking for it.

Google AdWords' Keyword Tool

The Google Adwords Keyword Tool is one of the weakest tools in terms of providing data you can rely on, yet remains one of the most popular keyword research tools online, because it still adds value if you understand how to interrupt the data.

The tool can be accessed at https://adwords.google.com/select/Keyword-ToolExternal where you can input either keywords, such as those you want to investigate or use as a starting point, or a website address, either your own or a competitor's. The tool will then return the keywords you searched for, along with other suggestions made by Google, such as synonyms, or related keywords that it believes are closely linked.

At this point, you will want to bear in mind the differences between Broad, Phrase and Exact match keywords as explained earlier in the book and either interpret the information accordingly, or set the tool to only use Exact match data (note that the tool is set to Broad match by default, giving you very high volume figures).

Once you know which keywords are being included in the volume data, you can then set the various columns to show you the information that you desire by clicking "Columns" near the upper right hand corner and selecting those which are most valuable to your current decision. The following screenshot shows that columns you can choose from, but again I suggest you click around to find your favorites.

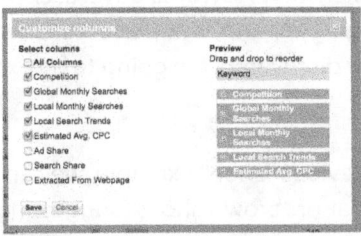

Image 5- Google AdWord's Keyword Tool column customization

It is again important to understand what is and isn't included in each of these pieces of data. The actual volume of searches listed under "Global Monthly Searches" is a 12-month average of the searches that took place, which means that it is not as helpful for highly cyclical markets. It is, therefore, important to note the small indication towards monthly fluctuations in search volume given within the diagram under "Local Search Trends," to understand if you should look at these cycles in greater detail.

Keyword	Competition	Estimated Avg. CPC	Global Monthly Searches	Local Monthly Searches	Local Search Trends
[shoes]		$0.93	368,000	165,000	
[brown shoes]		$0.49	6,600	1,600	
[socks]		$0.78	49,500	14,800	
[dress socks]		$1.95	1,300	590	

Image 6- Google AdWord's Keyword Tool results for Shoe based keywords

As an example, above, we can see that the volume of "shoes" is about 60—100 times larger than "brown shoes" both globally and locally, and that it was most searched between the months of March and May, whereas "socks" are most searched for in December.

In addition to these columns, I also usually select the "Competition" and "Estimated Avg. CPC (Cost per click)" columns when looking at AdWords data. This information is solely based on PPC data, but by seeing the average price being paid and the amount of competition I can get a fair understanding of the value of one keyword compared to another. There are many factors that might go into an AdWords advertiser paying more or less for a word, but the most important of these is the likelihood that they will buy a product, and the value of that transaction.

We can then use this information to add to our estimations for consumer intent and to better understand which are the most valuable keywords to rank for. As stated earlier, it is unlikely that AdWords advertisers are paying more for these terms than they are bringing in, and in a perfect market, any keywords that are cheaper than their value, if discovered, are going to be exploited and targeted until they reach an equal price.

Returning to the previous "shoe" example, we can see the term "shoes" has a CPC of almost double that of "brown shoes" suggesting that these searchers are either more likely to make a purchase, or when they do purchase it is more valuable to the businesses profits.

Microsoft Advertising Intelligence—Excel Plug-in

Behind Google, Microsoft, who owns Bing, which also powers Yahoo, is the next biggest search engine, and also provide their own tools for keyword research. One of these is Ad Intelligence, which is an Excel plug in that unfortunately only runs on Windows. This tool can be downloaded from http://advertising.microsoft.com/learning-center/adcenter-downloads/microsoft-advertising-intelligence and requires an adCenter account, which is free to set up and maintain, so long as you don't buy any PPC advertising.

Once installed within Excel, you will be given a new tab of options along the top of the page called 'adIntelligence' where you are given a number of options. Each of these options provides different types of data on keywords, some of which was looked at in the previous chapter, such as the "Demographic" tab to see the age and gender of those behind a keyword search.

Another area where this tool can be very useful is in the traffic section of the tool as it can provide a second set of data to compare with that from Google. The following screenshot shows this information for various "laptop" keywords.

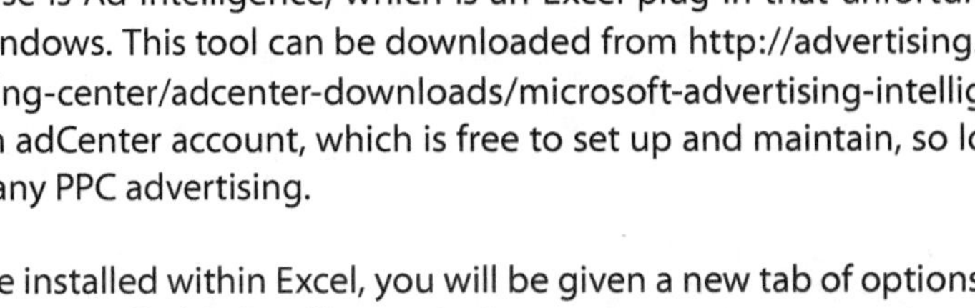

Keyword	Oct-09	Nov-09	Dec-09	Jan-10	Feb-10	Mar-10	Apr-10	May-10	Jun-10	Jul-10	Aug-10	Sep-10
laptop computers	74,718	137,185	92,738	29,358	17,019	230,484	15,181	14,892	14,082	21,888	64,336	14,
laptop	394,285	896,884	903,774	524,173	201,349	119,000	62,257	96,221	71,427	250,898	301,138	387,
laptops	152,798	415,806	249,251	76,254	185,068	167,490	258,586	118,653	51,918	135,158	112,279	167,
notebook computer	990	1,753	1,655	1,095	918	917	798	874	823	2,212	1,000	
notebook computers	4,370	6,737	6,949	4,163	3,197	3,500	3,149	4,384	4,255	4,296	3,831	3,
buy laptop	384	583	526	429	395	679	728	779	1,460	2,149	686	
computer	60,405	75,549	61,311	56,872	52,221	39,585	38,459	58,755	34,920	33,225	50,746	44,
desktop computer	2,765	3,478	5,062	3,142	3,185	3,547	2,433	2,349	3,165	3,388	3,499	2,

Image 7- Ad Intelligence data for laptop based keywords

Once again, it is important to note that it isn't so much the numbers themselves that are of value, but the patterns that are displayed within the data. For example, if both AdWords and Ad Intelligence show that one keyword has higher search volume than another, then you can use this information to select the keyword with larger search volume, with greater confidence in your findings. Similarly you can look at the traffic data over the past 12 months to look for trends and cycles and correlate these with the data from AdWords to understand any cycles or differences.

In addition, using the various functions listed across the top toolbar you can use many other features of this tool, all within Excel, which allows you to break up and analyze the data without ever changing programs. One of these useful features is the Keyword Extraction tool which can extract keywords from a current website, such as the following report for bestbuy.com:

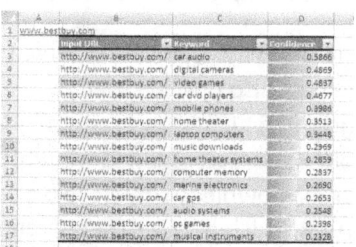

Image 8- Ad Intelligence data for keywords on bestbuy.com

Another useful feature is the Keyword Suggestion tool that offers other possible related keywords based on those you enter, ordered by the tools confidence in them being similar:

Image 9—Ad Intelligence data for suggested keywords related to "laptop computers"

These lists of keywords can be useful to suggest new keywords to you to further research that you may not have considered previously.

By themselves, none of these tools or reports provide much additional functionality compared to AdWords, although the interface and being able to use it within Excel is a handy feature. However, the ability to compare the data, and get information from a separate source, can greatly help a company in selecting keywords. You can obtain greater confidence in your findings, and even discover new options that were not returned by the first tool.

I would greatly recommend using both Ad Intelligence and AdWords in combination to gather preliminary data from both Google and Microsoft, helping you make a more accurate decision.

Competitor's Keywords

Another great place to begin compiling a list of possible keywords to evaluate is from your competitor's websites, and there are a number of ways and tools that can help you do this, like the Keyword Extraction tool shown previously.

Copying a competitor's keywords can be as simple as looking at their website and trying to get an idea of the keywords that they are targeting based on the words they are using within the page titles, heading tags, content, images and so on. However, a more effective way to do this is to use a tool such as SEMrush.com.

For the purposes of this example we will again use bestbuy.com, which retrieves the following information:

Organic keywords - 225,624

Keyword	Pos	Δ Volume	CPC	URL	Traffic %	Costs %	Competition	Results	Trend
best buy	1	12,274,040	0.90	bestbuy.com/	13.08	6.19	3.96	825,000,000	
laptops	1	3,697,000	5.22	bestbuy.com/site/Com...cat0502000	3.93	10.82	1.08	400,000,000	
best buy	2	12,274,040	0.90	bestbuy.com/site/ols...d=cat12090	3.61	1.71	3.96	825,000,000	
laptop computers	1	2,476,990	6.62	bestbuy.com/site/Com...cat0502000	2.63	9.19	2.68	48,600,000	
bestbuy	1	2,025,956	1.05	bestbuy.com/	2.15	1.19	3.58	3,860,000	

Full Report (225,624) »

AdWords keywords - 50,997

Ad	Keyword	Pos	Δ Volume	CPC	URL	Traffic %	Costs %	Competition	Results	Trend
	nintendo ds	1	2,476,990	0.60	www.BestBuy.com	5.88	2.52	3.70	82,700,000	
	digital camera	1	2,476,990	1.38	www.BestBuy.com	5.88	5.80	1.03	131,000,000	
	ps3	2	5,534,767	0.66	www.BestBuy.com	3.63	1.71	7.03	702,000,000	
	juegos	1	1,353,102	0.31	www.BestBuy.com/Espanol	3.21	0.71	2.78	109,000,000	
	ipod	3	5,530,712	1.44	www.BestBuy.com	2.51	2.58	7.03	182,000,000	

Full Report (50,997) »

Image 10—Organic and AdWords keywords sending traffic to bestbuy.com

This screenshot shows the top 5 keywords for both SEO and PPC, and you can click further for full reports. You again need to be fully aware of what this information is telling you, and how you can make this actionable for your own website. Organic keywords are those sending traffic via SEO, so are more a function of where the website currently ranks than the terms they necessarily want to rank for, or the terms that are sending them the most sales. This is why it is useful to look at AdWords keywords even if you plan on using these only for SEO, as these are the terms that tell us the traffic BestBuy considers most valuable and highly converting, as well as the approximate cost per click they are paying.

However, just because a keyword is working well for your competitor doesn't mean it will necessarily work well for you, based on your website, selection and your own business's strengths. Similarly, terms such as "best buy" or "bestbuy" will never be worth targeting for a competitor due to this being a navigational search query rather than a user searching to buy a specific product.

Another useful tool that you can also use to look at competitor's websites is Alexa (www.alexa.com) where you can then access their "Site Information" for information on keywords as well as a wide range of other data including traffic estimates.

Again, in the case of Best Buy, you can see their various most popular key-words, this time not distinguished between organic or PPC, as well as the amount of traffic they receive from search results compared to site wide volumes:

Image 11—Alexa information for bestbuy.com

Using this information, which does differ slightly with that from the previous tools, you can again get an understanding on where your competitors are, where their focus is, and how each term might be affecting their bottom line. It is then a business decision that you will have to make as to whether they are truly leading the market and you should follow; or if their efforts in the field are below what they could be, providing you with a very valuable opportunity to invest in SEO and steal market share away from them.

Website Analytics

In addition to the information you are able to obtain about your competitors, you should also have vast amounts of website analytics information for your own site possibly dating back several years. There are many programs that you might use to measure your web analytics, which goes beyond the scope of this book, but the most popular is Google Analytics, which will be the main focus in both this section, and also later in the book when it comes to measuring your selected keywords.

Assuming your analytics tool has been set up correctly, with accurate goals and goal values, this information can give you a much stronger understanding of the value of keywords to your business, and the probability that visitors using these terms will convert into paying customers and how much they might spend.

With keyword research and web analytics you can quantify exactly how many customers are coming to your website from searches for each of your prod-ucts, what they want to know about it and what they do when they find it. You can learn how long it takes for them to make a decision; did they buy a different product than they originally searched for? What is the conversion rate of traffic searching for different keywords? All of this information, and much more, can be discovered through gathering and analyzing keyword research and using it along-side your website analytics data.

Looking at the web analytics for VerticalMeasures.com, with the keywords themselves blurred out for privacy reasons, you can see the goal information available for the top 10 keywords sending the most traffic by volume:

	Keyword	None	Visits	Goal Conversion Rate	Per Visit Goal Value
1.			222	4.05%	$2.79
2.			184	4.89%	$4.35
3.			180	3.33%	$2.28
4.			142	3.52%	$3.17
5.			122	0.00%	$0.00
6.			66	0.00%	$0.00
7.			52	3.85%	$3.85
8.			39	0.00%	$0.00
9.			38	2.63%	$0.26
10.			33	0.00%	$0.00

Image 12—Google Analytics keyword report

What we can then gather from this information is that keywords 1—4, as well as currently providing the most traffic, all have some of the best per visit goal values, meaning that they are the visitors most likely to convert into sales on our website. The second term is the most valuable to the business, meaning that our SEO budget might be best placed on focusing on improving rankings for this keyword compared to those with lower goal conversion rates.

However, you can also see that we get very little conversions from terms 5, 6 and 8-10. It could be the case that these keywords seem to be the most attractive to a business based on other keyword tools showing high volume and intent, but the fact is that these are not shown to be converting well into sales on our site. We, therefore, know not to focus resources into these terms, regardless of what the various tools tell us. (It should be said that we could focus on better converting these terms by rewriting content and changing landing page design etc., but this is beyond the scope of this book).

Depending on the analytics software you are using, you may then be able to analyze what each piece of traffic did on your website, the pages they looked at, the information they were after, and if they later returned to your website to make a purchase at a later date. Armed with this information you can then dig deeper into understanding each searcher's intent when they come to your website, and how you can satisfy their needs as best as possible.

The one thing that is very important to note when using previous web analytics data to determine future keywords is that this information, particularly the number of visits, is an indication of where the website currently stands, not where it can be in the future. You will want to focus primarily on the most valuable keywords based on conversion percentages, not those with the highest volumes, as this will tell you the potential gains that can be realized by ranking highly, not just the current picture.

Keyword Difficulty

Finding the volume for keywords, and their ability to convert into sales, is, however, only half the battle. As we saw previously in the "Factors to Consider" chapter, a large portion of the decision is going to depend on internal factors such as budget and the strength of your current website. It is a fair assumption that more competitive terms are going to require a more optimized website to rank highly, and ultimately a larger budget.

However, working out the competitiveness of a keyword can be difficult and there are a number of various factors you can look at separately. Alternatively, you can use the SeoMoz Keyword Difficulty tool at http://www.seomoz.org/keyword-difficulty/. As with all of their tools, access to this does require a PRO membership, so it isn't free, but this does give you access to all of their other incredibly useful tools.

Within this tool you can enter up to five keywords to see their competitiveness, given to you as a percentage figure, making it quick and easy to get an idea of a terms competitiveness. Although this can range anywhere between 0-100%, I have never seen it much below 40%, without it being a long tail term (a keyword with four or more words, such as "nike high top basketball shoes"), or really any higher than 75%, so you can use these figures to get a better idea of a term's competitiveness.

For example, if your term has a competitiveness of 25%, you know you could probably rank well for the term with very little investment and optimization, whereas a term of 75% difficulty might take months of link building and many thousands of dollars.

In the screenshot below, you can see the information returned for five completely different keywords. Although the tool also returns volume numbers from the AdWords API, it is only really the first column we are interested in here:

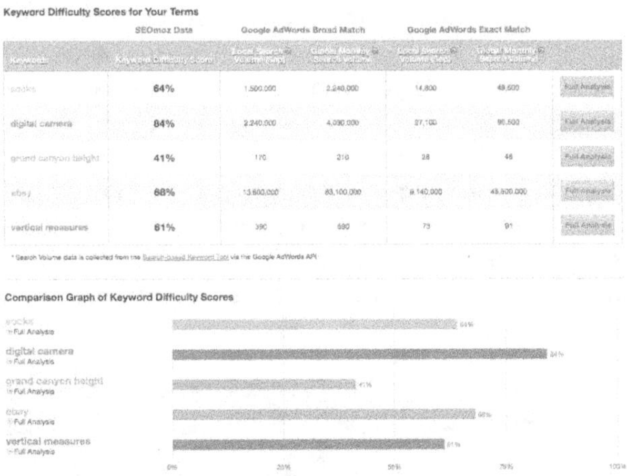

Image 13- SeoMoz Keyword Difficulty report

From this information we can see that the two transactional terms of "socks" and "digital camera" are very competitive, especially digital camera presumably because of the higher value of the product, and the likelihood of consumers to buy this product online.

Similarly, of the two navigational terms "ebay" is more competitive than "vertical measures" because of the larger popularity of searchers looking for this term and its commercial benefit.

Finally the informational query of "grand canyon height" has the lowest competition due to its non-commercial intent, and very low volume, meaning that very few websites would target this term, but those that did could rank fairly easily.

While this information alone can help you understand the competition for terms you may wish to target, it is important to understand where this tool is getting its information. SeoMoz looks at the authority of the pages ranking in the top ten results in Google for these search queries and ranks a term's competitiveness based on the quality of these sites. This means that those websites might not be directly targeting those terms (search for "click here" to see a live example), meaning you might be able to outrank them with a targeted effort. However, this is a very useful tool that can give you a quick snapshot of many different ranking factors.

MSN Commercial Intent

In addition to the Excel Plug In, Microsoft offers a range of online tools available at http://adlab.msn.com/, some of which are included in the plug in itself, such as Demographic data, and some which where excluded. One such example of these tools that was not included in the Excel plug in and yet is very useful is the Commercial Intent tool that you can access at http://adlab.msn.com/Online-Commercial-Intention/.

By entering a keyword into the tool, you are given the probability that the searcher looking for a particular URL or search query is looking to make a purchase. For example, as shown below you can see that the tool is 99% sure that "digital camera" is a transactional query, whereas it is 84% sure that "photograph" is not going to result in a purchase:

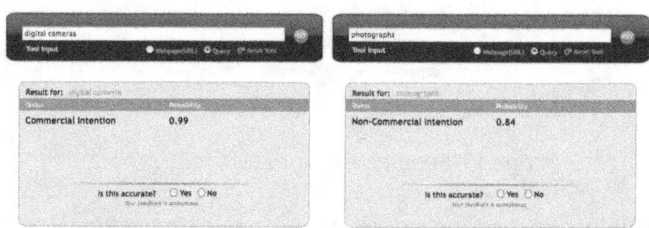

Image 14- Microsoft Ad Intelligence for 'digital cameras' and 'photographs'

Depending on the results and the search queries themselves, this tool can help your keyword research and ensure that you are targeting terms that will add to your business's bottom line. In this example, the term "photograph" might be too vague to lead to any kind of purchase, and might be considered an informational or action keyword query.

Returning to two previous examples earlier in this book, this tool might be the first indication to a website performing keyword research that despite what you might initially think, "engagement ring" and "ferarri" in fact have low commercial intent, as they are predominantly searched by those who are simply looking and dreaming. It would, therefore, not be wise to base a business on making sales from this audience.

The website providing this tool claims that the intent was calculated algo-rithmically, meaning that perhaps they tracked online transactions following these searches. This, of course, means that they would have neglected to consider any offline transactions that followed as a result, or perhaps longer sales cycles where the consumer returned to the website directly to make a purchase, so it is again important to consider the data behind each tool as well as your business goals and its industry.

SERP Results and Current Rankings

As stated with the previous tool, knowing the "keyword difficulty" for any keyword is not necessarily enough to help you decide between keywords and understand what it might take to rank well for a term. As the SeoMoz tool is based only on the pages that are currently ranking and doesn't take into account if they are purposefully targeting these terms, it is sometimes necessary to go a step further and look at the actual SERP results and current rankings.

You can begin this process by searching a possible keyword in Google, or another search engine you want to evaluate, and then looking at the pages that currently rank highly for that term. If it appears that many of these pages are not particularly focused on that keyword—for example they don't include it within the page title or content—you can assume that it would not be too difficult to rank highly for that keyword with a well-optimized webpage.

However, more often than not, the pages that do rank for any commercial keyword will at least be well targeted towards these terms and include the keywords in the page title, content, url etc (as shown in bold in the below example):

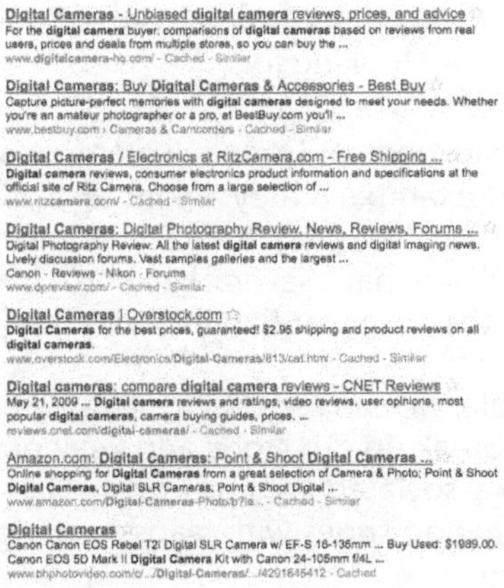
Digital Cameras - Unbiased **digital camera** reviews, prices, and advice
For the **digital camera** buyer: comparisons of **digital cameras** based on reviews from real users, prices and deals from multiple stores, so you can buy the ...
www.digitalcamera-hq.com/ - Cached - Similar

Digital Cameras: Buy **Digital Cameras** & Accessories - Best Buy
Capture picture-perfect memories with **digital cameras** designed to meet your needs. Whether you're an amateur photographer or a pro, at BestBuy.com you'll ...
www.bestbuy.com › Cameras & Camcorders - Cached - Similar

Digital Cameras / Electronics at RitzCamera.com - Free Shipping ...
Digital camera reviews, consumer electronics product information and specifications at the official site of Ritz Camera. Choose from a large selection of ...
www.ritzcamera.com/ - Cached - Similar

Digital Cameras: Digital Photography Review, News, Reviews, Forums ...
Digital Photography Review: All the latest **digital camera** reviews and digital imaging news. Lively discussion forums. Vast samples galleries and the largest ...
Canon - Reviews - Nikon - Forums
www.dpreview.com/ - Cached - Similar

Digital Cameras | Overstock.com
Digital Cameras for the best prices, guaranteed! $2.95 shipping and product reviews on all **digital cameras**.
www.overstock.com/Electronics/**Digital-Cameras**/813/cat.html - Cached - Similar

Digital cameras: compare **digital camera** reviews - CNET Reviews
May 21, 2009 ... **Digital camera** reviews and ratings, video reviews, user opinions, most popular **digital cameras**, camera buying guides, prices, ...
reviews.cnet.com/**digital-cameras**/ - Cached - Similar

Amazon.com: **Digital Cameras**: Point & Shoot **Digital Cameras** ...
Online shopping for **Digital Cameras** from a great selection of Camera & Photo; Point & Shoot **Digital Cameras**, Digital SLR Cameras, Point & Shoot Digital ...
www.amazon.com/**Digital-Cameras**-Photo/b?ie ... - Cached - Similar

Digital Cameras
Canon Canon EOS Rebel T2i Digital SLR Camera w/ EF-S 18-135mm ... Buy Used: $1989.00. Canon EOS 5D Mark II **Digital Camera** Kit with Canon 24-105mm f/4L ...
www.bhphotovideo.com/c/.../**Digital-Cameras**/.../4291645412 - Cached

Image 15- SERP for keyword 'digital cameras'

You can then investigate these webpages in terms of other offsite factors to evaluate how difficult they may be to over take in the rankings. By looking at factors such as PageRank and using tools like Open Site Explorer, as explained previously, to look at number of links, quality of links, anchor text etc, and comparing this to your own site, you can gain a fair understanding of the time and budget needed to achieve high rankings for this keyword.

Another important factor that shouldn't be overlooked when reviewing your current SERPs is your own website's ranking for a keyword. You may not have considered this keyword before, meaning you haven't even been tracking your ranking, yet still be positioned somewhere on page 3 or 4 or perhaps higher. If this is the case, this is another indication that you may be able to rank quickly for this term with less investment than if you are not within the first 10 pages of results.

You should also take into consideration the page of your site that is being returned and leverage this for your future efforts, using this URL when building a keyword strategy and content, as discussed in the next chapter.

Google Instant, Suggest and Related Queries

Continuing from analyzing the current SERPs and the information that Google and other search engines return, there are many visual clues within the result pages themselves that can also be used for keyword discovery and research.

In the past year, Google in particular added a Suggest feature to its search bar, which in the past few months has expanded into Google Instant. What these features essentially do it try to guess what you are searching for so that you don't have to type in the entire words and can simply choose the term you want from a drop down menu. For example, just by typing "exp", Google will suggest expedia as that is most likely what you are looking for.

Aside from the implications of Google Instant, and how this might change the way people search (for example if they are more likely to search for suggested terms or continue typing their preferred phrase) this information can be very valuable for keyword research. If you have several keywords in mind, you can type these into Google and see what they suggest that includes this phrase.

In the below example, we can see that if we ran an online store selling dress shoes, we might want to break up our store, and keyword focus by gender. In addition, depending on the associated volumes, you could maybe write blog posts about inflamed feet, or wearing shoes with jeans assuring them that it is comfortable, and it does look good.

dress shoes	×	Search
dress shoes		
dress shoes for women		
dress shoes for men		
dress shoes for plantar fasciitis		
dress shoes with jeans		

Image 16- Google Suggest for 'dress shoes'

Scroll even further down the page and you will see a selection of related searches at the very bottom. Both this, and the above information come from a Google algorithm that looks for patterns in how people search. For example, it might be that searchers find the results of "dress shoes" too generic and then specify their searches for "mens dress shoes" or "discount dress shoes." Google then suggests these options to help you search more quickly;

Searches related to **dress shoes**

special occasion shoes	dillards
evening shoes	prom dress shoes
mens dress shoes	payless shoes
discount dress shoes	mens shoes

Gooooooooogle ▶

1 2 3 4 5 6 7 8 9 10   Next

Image 17- Related searches for "dress shoes"

You can then use all of these keyword suggestions, as well as similar ones from http://soovle.com/ and http://suggest.thinkpragmatic.net/ and return back to the AdWords Keyword Tool, MSN Excel plug-in and other tools, to work out intent and search volumes to evaluate how good these terms may be for success.

Google Wonder Wheel

Before we leave the Google search pages, there is another option available that shows similar data to the above by displaying related search terms, known as the Wonder Wheel. The Wonder Wheel can be found by doing any search and selecting "more search tools" in the left hand navigation and then choosing "Wonder Wheel" under the heading "Standard View". You are then shown a wonderful wheel that visualizes any connected keywords, which you can click further to see even more related terms:

Image 18- Wonder Wheel result for "dress shoes" and then "mens dress shoes"

As you can see, the words on the first wheel are very similar to those given at the bottom of the results page for related terms, but the fact that you can click to see further related terms is a useful feature that adds a small element of fun to keyword research.

This tool is great for digging deeper into niche areas of a product, and can also be very useful for finding supplementary, complementary and competing products that your website may not currently offer, but could easily expand into. You may also be able to discover the keywords that enable you to target your consumer either earlier or later in the buying cycle.

Google Insights for Search and Google Trends

Finally, the last couple of tools that are also offered by Google have already been mentioned earlier in this book under a couple of the factors to consider and are "Insights for Search" and "Trends." Both of these tools show similar sets of information, with Insights for Search digging a little deeper, so we shall look at the more simple "Trends" first.

Google Trends is available at http://www.google.com/trends and this is where you are able to see information on whether or not a market is growing or in decline (based on searches for a term) as well as see any cyclicality to the searches being made. Simply enter in the search term, or several terms separated by commas, to see the data for those queries.

You are then returned various pieces of data displayed in a manner similar to the following, which for this example compares the searches for "itunes" with "cd":

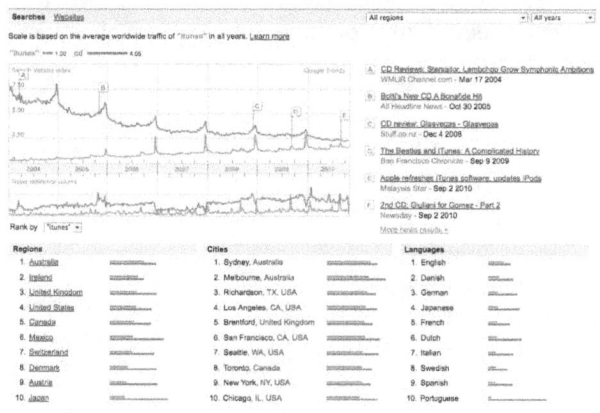

Image 19- Google Trends data for "itunes" (blue) and "cd" (red)

Given the name of the tool, as you might expect, in the main chart in the top left you can see the overall trend for a keyword over the past 7 years. All numbers that are shown in these results are indexed against the value of 1.00, and are not true search volume figures, but offer a way to see how the volume changes over time and across different regions, as opposed to exact volume figures.

In this instance you can see that the term "cd" has fallen dramatically since 2004 while "itunes" has grown steadily, albeit at a slower rate. This data could tell a music company that while iTunes seems to have replaced buying music on discs, this isn't necessarily the case as CDs still beat "itunes" in terms of search volume.

However, a company should also take into account the fact that "itunes" need only be searched one time to download the program, and also consider the various other meanings of the term "cd" to get a complete idea of what the data means.

Also shown on this graph are any news items that may have sparked large changes in search volume for either term, shown in the top right, helping you see how an industry can be affected by changes in the economy.

Finally, the bottom row of data shows how search volumes change across different countries, cities and languages. These are listed in order of the highest volume for the first search term you entered, and their bar graphs show data indexed against the first keyword. In this example we can see that the English language dominates the results as well as English-speaking countries, perhaps suggesting that other cultures still prefer their music in CD format.

Building on this Trends data, Google has also developed "Insights for Search" -http://www.google.com/insights/search—which provides similar functionality with a few extra built in features. By changing some of the options in the screenshot below, you are able to see things such as the top searches in a particular time frame, or the most popular searches in a country. However, for keyword market research this isn't exactly useful, so you will instead want to focus on just using the "Compare by Search terms" function.

You are then free to change all of the other options, to focus particularly on Web search, or Images, News or Products, and focus on particular time frames, countries, regions and sub-regions. The information that returns is organized similarly to Trends, and once again shows comparisons rather than actual search volumes. However, there is one useful feature that can help in focusing your efforts in the right markets, which is the map;

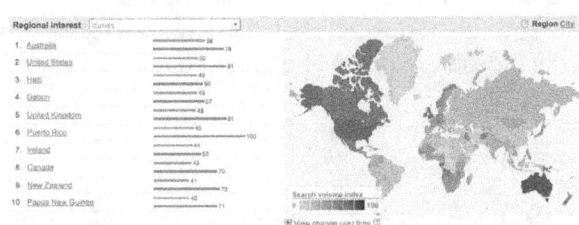

Image 20- Google Insights for Search Map for "itunes" searches

This map shows the areas with the greatest activity in a darker blue, and is also fully interactive, allowing you to look within the countries for the most active regions, making it useful for finding keywords for a local search campaign and perhaps assisting your offline marketing in the areas that are most interested in certain products. In this example, we can again see how the English speaking countries seem to have the greatest searches for "itunes", but you can also see the areas that stand out from those around them, such as both Afghanistan and Iraq in the above map.

Finally, Insights also provides a look at popular related terms, and how they compare, as well as terms that grew greatly in popularity during the time frame selected. The information below is using the keyword of "dress shoes" to show how this data compares to the previous suggest tools:

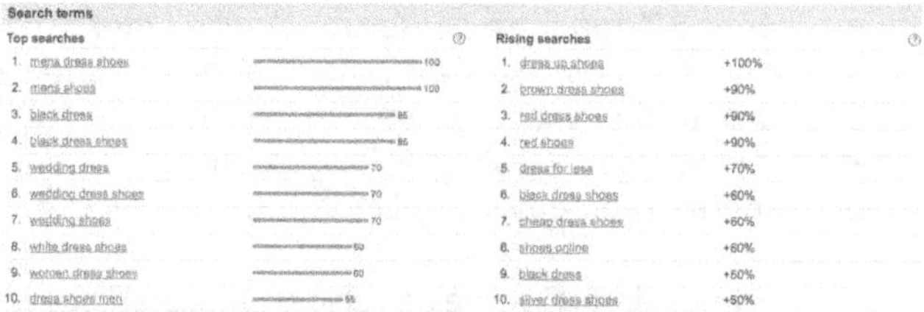

Search terms

Top searches		Rising searches	
1. mens dress shoes	100	1. dress up shoes	+100%
2. mens shoes	100	2. brown dress shoes	+90%
3. black dress	85	3. red dress shoes	+90%
4. black dress shoes	85	4. red shoes	+90%
5. wedding dress	70	5. dress for less	+70%
6. wedding dress shoes	70	6. black dress shoes	+60%
7. wedding shoes	70	7. cheap dress shoes	+60%
8. white dress shoes	60	8. shoes online	+60%
9. women dress shoes	60	9. black dress	+50%
10. dress shoes men	55	10. silver dress shoes	+50%

Image 21- Google Insights for Search Top and Rising Searches related to "dress shoes"

As with the previous couple of tools, you can see a selection of related keywords on the left hand side, and how they compare to "dress shoes" which would have a volume of 100, as this is how the tool indexes the volume data. However, the most interesting data is on the right hand side where we can see that searches for "brown" and "red", "cheap" and "for less" are up in popularity hugely over the time period selected.

This kind of data is particularly important for fashion or technology websites where the products in demand are constantly changing. Being able to see rising popularity searches before your competition can put your business at a great competitive advantage and again shows the value of keyword research as wider market research within your industry to get the hottest trends directly from what your customers are looking to buy.

Other Research Tools

That concludes this portion of the book where I aimed to highlight some of the tools I use most often in performing keyword research and how the data they each return can be used to provide any extra information on keywords you may be considering. At the beginning of this chapter I stated that I did not want this to be a "how to" but that you should have enough information to start using these tools yourself to start making better keyword decisions.

However, I should again state that this list is by no means exhaustive, and new keyword tools are being released seemingly all the time by various SEO and SEM related websites. While these tools are the ones that I use most often this doesn't mean that they are necessarily the best, just that I am comfortable using them and have a strong level of understanding of how to interrupt the data they are returning. I would suggest that you research other tools that may better fit the way you think or the information you wish to discover.

As a starting point to this process, below is a list of some of the other tools in the industry, and what they can be useful for, that where left out of this book either for brevity or because their functions are not vastly different to others that were included:

Trellian Keyword Discovery—http://www.keyworddiscovery.com/
> The keyword discovery tool provides consolidated data from the major search engines all in one place. With a membership cost between $70 and $200 a month it can perform the features of many tools all in one place included finding related terms, volumes and trends.

Hitwise Search Intelligence—http://www.hitwise.com/us
> Hitwise is only a viable option for the biggest businesses out there and can cost many thousands of dollars a year, depending on your individual needs, business size, access and so on. However, if you do have access, it provides great functionality allowing you to directly compare keywords to one another, and perform gap analysis to discover areas of the market you are currently ignoring.

Wordstream—http://www.wordstream.com
> Wordstream has a suite of completely free keyword research tools that between them can discover, suggest, group and otherwise analyze many aspects of keywords. The data comes from a number of sources to provide greater accuracy, and the thousands of results that are returned can be downloaded directly for you to analyze in a spreadsheet, which is a useful feature.

WordTracker—http://www.wordtracker.com
> WordTracker comes at a price of $60 a month and again provides similar functionality to discover new keywords and analyze their relevant data. However, WordTracker also has a labs section for their beta tools, which includes http://labs.wordtracker.com/keyword-questions, a

great tool for finding questions based around your keywords. This is useful for writing content and generating ideas for blog post topics.

Microsoft AdLab Keyword Mutation—http://adlab.msn.com/Keyword-Mutation-Detection

While you may feel like performing some keyword mutation yourself by this point, this tool in fact tells you some common misspellings and errors performed by searchers. I would not recommend that you target these terms directly on your site, for the sake of brand professionalism, but by including them in your page meta keywords or links to your website, you can rank for these queries also to drive additional traffic.

SpyFu—http://www.spyfu.com

SpyFu does as the name suggests, and allows you to spy on your competitors. You can see their keywords for both organic traffic and PPC, similar to SEM Rush, see their budget and download all of the data to make better decisions for your own business.

Yahoo Clues—http://clues.yahoo.com

A new tool that provides a lot of data in one location based around a keyword's trends over time, most popular locations and demographic information similar to that provided by Insights for Search as well as the Microsoft adCenter.

BUILDING A KEYWORD STRATEGY

So, you've thought about your business's online goals, and, therefore, the important elements of keywords you may wish to target, and you've collected all of the necessary data. By now you probably have several spreadsheets and notes for a range of different keywords and competitors. You hopefully learned something about your target audience, who searches for what online and how you can optimize your website content and structure accordingly. You may have even learnt that the traffic you have been focusing on for years isn't the best kind of traffic out there for your business.

So now what do you do? Now comes the most important part—you have to pick the actual keywords that your business is actually going to target for the foreseeable future with either an SEO or PPC campaign. This means you have to also work on designing the rest of your business and its website accordingly based on this target audience and what you have learnt about them.

With PPC it can be easy to select keywords, try them for a while to see their traffic and sales returns, and then either carry on or end the campaign—depending on results and other variables such as advert copy and landing page.

However, SEO is focused more on the long term and it can take several months to rank for your chosen keyword terms, meaning that you don't actually know the value of the keyword until it is almost too late. This means that keyword selection is a vital decision and you must select the best possible keywords to put your online business on the right path for success. You will need to carefully weigh all of the options you have researched and select the terms that you believe can help you reach your goals.

For most businesses aiming for sales, you will need to consider the volume and consumer intent, i.e. the number of possible sales, versus the difficulty to rank for that term in regards to both time and money. For other businesses looking for traffic or branding, this formula will be different and might be more focused on long tail or informational terms to bring in related traffic.

Furthermore, you may wish to target some of the easiest wins in a market, the terms that you can rank for in a short amount of time but that have low volume so that you are able to bootstrap your business and reinvest the money from these sales to target the big terms later down the line. Alternatively, you may have the budget to target these terms head on, sacrificing short-term returns for a larger future return on investment.

As you can see, there are nearly endless possibilities and scenarios depending on every unique business and industry. It is because of all of these different elements that make both businesses and keywords uniquely different from each other, that no one formula for selecting the right terms could ever be produced. However, after you spend some time looking at the various terms, and as you gain knowledge of an industry, you can learn to identify what is most important to your business, and start to pick out the keywords that you want to focus on.

You can then use these chosen keywords to construct a keyword strategy and start to bring in some of this targeted search traffic.

Choosing Keywords

Depending on the size of your budget or website, the size of the list of chosen keywords you want to target can vary greatly. For the purposes of this example, lets say that this figure is between 20 and 30 keywords. These keywords will be those from the several hundred you researched in the previous phase of the process that offered you the greatest chance for success.

For most businesses this will be the terms with the best combination of volume, consumer intent and low competition, such as those in the 3 and 4 word "sweet spot".

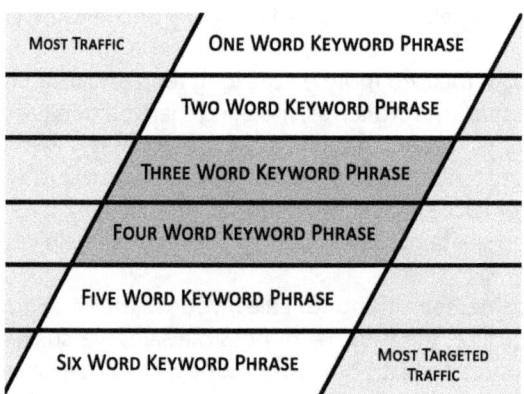

Table 22—Traffic volume versus commercial intent, adapted from http://www.poleposition marketing.com/library/ebooks/keyword-research.pdf

Armed with this list of your selected keywords, you should group these terms based on their similarities so that all similar terms are with each other, such as those related to the same products, or sharing similar searcher intent. For example, an online coffee retailer might group all of their espresso together, their gourmet coffee in one group, and their decaf in another and so on.

The next step is to break down each of these groups into smaller subsets of between 2 and 4 keywords in each subset. These subsets will ultimately represent pages on your website that will target these 2 to 4 keywords, so the more related these keywords are, the easier page content creation will be.

You will want to target fewer keywords per page if they are more competitive, but no more than 4 on any page, including plural and singular variations, to keep these pages focused. To continue the example of an online coffee retailer, they might ultimately end up with a table such this:

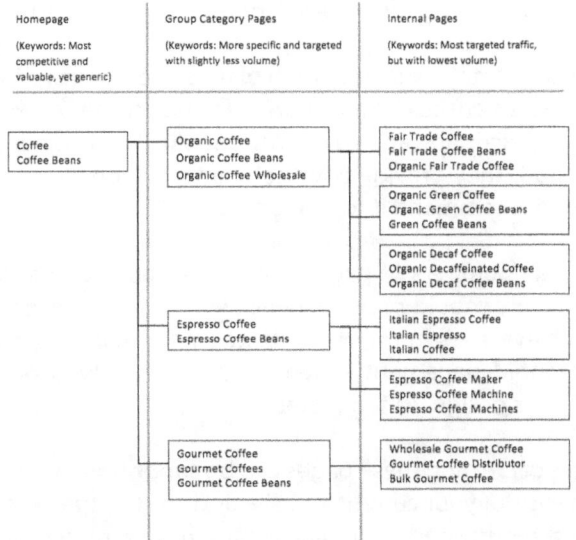

Table 10—Sample keyword strategy for an online coffee retailer

This table then represents a logical structure for the website, with each box representing an individual webpage, and the keywords within it being the terms it would aim to rank for in the search engine results.

You would have only one homepage in the left hand column targeting the most competitive, valuable, generic keywords. This homepage would then lead to several category level pages in the middle column targeting more specific keywords, and each of these categories could have any number of pages and subcategories within them depending on your website, its market, and your selected keywords.

As you move further to the right, you should move to smaller keywords in terms of search volume that are probably longer tail terms, but terms that are more specific with a higher chance of conversion.

Content Planning

With a keyword strategy then laid out, you have a basis for your website structure and SEO or PPC campaign. The next step is to create the actual pages with relevant information that will correlate with the search query you want the page to rank for. For example, if the query is transactional in nature this will be a sales page where purchases can be made. Conversely an informational query will require a page that actually contains useful information about the topic that the searcher wanted to learn about (you could then use this is a chance to entice your visitor to a separate sales page once they have the information they wanted).

You will also want to ensure that each of these new pages is in line with other SEO guidelines, such as onsite optimization to include these keywords in the page title, heading tags, description and so on. You should also consider the "linkability" of these pages and if they provide any useful information that a related website might link to you to recommend it to its readers.

Creating large numbers of pages can be a difficult and a time consuming process, but ultimately should prove beneficial to not only correctly target a keyword, but also achieve sales from your website's visitors. It can also be supported with a good Content Management System (CMS), such as Wordpress, that can automate SEO and page design via templates.

The process of creating these pages can be supported by performing a complete content analysis of your current website and its structure to see what can be saved, reused and repurposed. You may already have a perfect piece of content about coffee machines, to continue the coffee retailer example, which can just be tweaked, moved and retargeted to successfully focus on a newly chosen keyword.

When writing your website content, you should consider all of the information and data you gathered during the previous two stages. You should have at your fingertips data that describes the demographics of the people who are likely to visit each page, other related information and searches they might be interested in, and the likelihood that they are wanting to make a purchase. This will help you to craft the tone of voice used across your different pages, the importance of a sales call to action on the website and related information that can keep them on your website and interested in your brand.

You can then take this process one step further to develop various "Search Personas", which is a way to group searcher behavior that you are hoping to attract to your website and provide them with the information they desire. These personas will differ by various aspects but most commonly will differ by the goal behind their search, their phase in the buying cycle, or their demographic information.

For any website the number of search personas can range from anything upwards from about five, but to further continue the example of an online coffee retailer three such personas may look like the following (adapted from Fox, *Marketing in the Age of Google*):

Searcher Goal	Target Search Queries	Task Completion	Business Goal
Find the right espresso machine for their needs and make a purchase	· Espresso Coffee Maker · Espresso Coffee Machine · Espresso Coffee Machines	Find and buy espresso machine	Develop a loyal customer that will buy espresso beans for the life of the machine.

Searcher Goal	Target Search Queries	Task Completion	Business Goal
Research and buy ethical coffee products	· Fair Trade Coffee · Fair Trade Coffee Beans · Organic Fair Trade Coffee	Buy fair trade coffee	Develop brand awareness and customer loyalty.

Searcher Goal	Target Search Queries	Task Completion	Business Goal
Find out the differences between coffee from different countries and types of roast	· Coffee beans same as espresso beans · Coffee beans highest in caffeine	Find answer to question	Create brand awareness. Subscribe to newsletter or mailing list.

Tables 11, 12, 13—Sample search personas for an online coffee retailer

You can then use these search personas to define how you will design each page, as well as its actual written content. For example, with the first search persona who are looking to buy their first espresso machine the website will look to introduce their brand and what it stands for. They could also try to gather information about their visitors, such as their email address, so that even if they don't buy a machine from them, they can stay in contact with the visitor and potentially become their life long coffee supplier.

Measuring Results

After spending so much time researching keywords, developing a keyword strategy and then producing every one of these webpages, you are going to, of course, want to measure the results. How you measure these results will again depend on the goals of the business and what you actually wanted to achieve. For example, was it branding and traffic volume, or just the number of sales? The answer to this question will define how you measure your return on investment (ROI), but ultimately you will once again want to return to your web analytics program.

Within your web analytics program you can then see the performance of each of your keywords, much the same as you could when looking at your previous keywords in the "Factors to Consider" chapter. The factors that are most likely to be important for your measurement of success are as follows:

- Pages Per Visit—Once the visitor has arrived to your website, how many pages do they view? Do visitors from certain keywords visit more pages than those from others and why? Is this because they found the information they were looking for or had to hunt to find it, or because they found the information they wanted but then wanted to learn more about your brand? Which pages do they go on to visit, and are they sales based?
- Average Time on Site—As with the above, are visitors from some keywords spending longer amounts of time on your site than others and why? Are certain keywords sending traffic that is likely to read and absorb information rather than quickly scanning your pages and moving on?
- Bounce Rate—The bounce rate simply refers to the number of visitors who leave your website after just one page. Depending on your business model this isn't necessarily a bad thing and could signal that they found the information they need, but many websites will aim for a low bounce rate for a keyword to signify that visitors are landing on the page and then continue to move through the website or complete an order.
- Conversion Rate—The most important criteria for measuring a keyword is likely to be the conversion rate itself, i.e. the number of visitors from that keyword who converted into a sale. If you have E-Commerce tracking you can then analyze this data further to see which keywords are sending the most profitable sales or those with the largest order size and so on. Furthermore, conversion rate isn't restricted just to sales, but can signify a visitor giving you their contact information or signing up to be a member.

	Keyword	None	Visits	Pages/Visit	Avg. Time on Site	% New Visits	Bounce Rate
1.			837	10.97	00:05:34	99.54%	12.40%
2.			567	14.90	00:07:33	71.60%	10.41%
3.			524	3.94	00:02:28	93.13%	36.26%
4.			418	7.87	00:03:46	88.84%	39.95%
5.			349	6.50	00:03:10	81.66%	34.38%
6.			340	6.11	00:02:13	93.24%	22.65%
7.			338	9.46	00:05:16	86.39%	19.82%
8.			258	7.54	00:04:08	86.82%	40.70%
9.			250	6.30	00:03:00	73.20%	32.00%

Image 23-Keyword report in Google Analytics

Using this information you can then calculate any return from these keywords in the manner most suitable for your business. This might include the number of visitors it sent, how many sales this lead to, how many loyal returning customers were obtained, what their live time value is and so on. Depending on your business model you may also wish to consider the changes in foot traffic that comes to your brick and mortar locations, the phone calls you receive, or the amount of traffic that comes to your website directly, although they may have found you via search initially.

The different reports and information available within a web analytics program is far beyond the scope of this book, but all of the information is available so that you can see the exact value of traffic you acquire as a result of each keyword you selected in the previous stage.

However, depending on your business goals, the ROI of a campaign, and the analysis of your chosen keywords is not limited to the performance of your website when visitors come, but also the actual number of visitors and the position in your rankings.

You might, therefore, wish to also keep a close eye on your rankings in search engines for your chosen keywords and compare this data to the invested budget over the same time period. If you have selected keywords with the right level of competition for your budget size, then you should see your rankings gradually increasing over time until you start to appear on page one and the traffic to your website from a keyword increases exponentially.

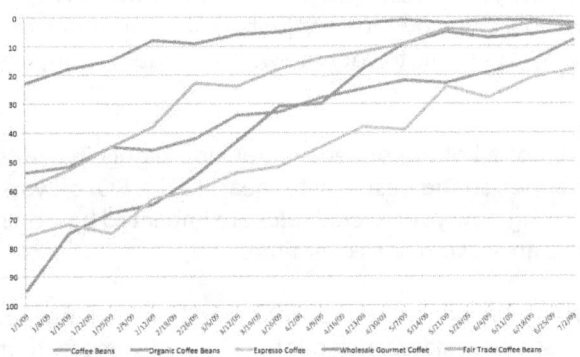

Image 24- Sample of tracking keyword rankings in a search engine

You can also use this ranking data to compare your estimates on keyword difficulty and the amount of investment needed to rank for a keyword with the reality. By measuring data in this way, the next time you do keyword research you will have a better idea of the information returned by each of the tools in Chapter 2, and how you can accurately interrupt the results for more accurate budgeting.

Furthermore, you can also use the data available in Google Webmaster Tools (www.google.com/webmasters/tools) to get an understanding of the number of times your website is being returned for various keywords, where it is positioned in the results and the number of visitors who ultimately click through to your website:

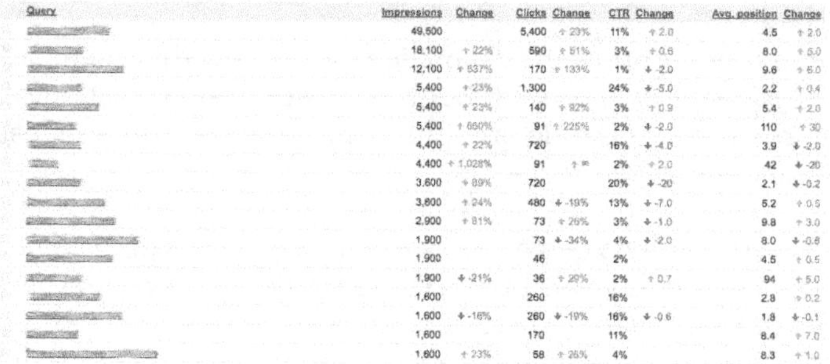

Image 25- Keyword report in Google Webmaster Tools

However, despite all of this data available at your fingertips, do not be too quick to judge SEO or PPC campaigns or change your keywords before they have had a chance to succeed. As has been discussed this can be a long-term effort that will not pay its dividends until you hit the first page of Google. It is not uncommon to see little return on your investment in the first few months, but so long as you continue to invest, once you do rank on the first page of results for a keyword you can see high numbers of traffic to your site without requiring any significant further investment.

In addition, not all of the benefits of ranking highly in SERPs are able to be tracked in this manner, so the best way to measure the ROI on your choice of key-words is by evaluating how your overall sales are impacted based on your keyword strategy, content plan and rankings over time.

Website visitors may find you through one keyword, but return directly to make a purchase at a later date. They might call you for more information having found you by an informational query, or they may even visit your brick and mortar location. All of these activities will be missed if you are evaluating your returns too narrowly, so try to be as all encompassing as possible when measuring the returns to avoid neglecting a highly performing keyword.

CONCLUSION

As you can see, there can be an almost overwhelming number of factors, tools and relationships involved in keyword research that can be somewhat daunting at first. In addition, the temptation to say "I know my customer" can be great and can lead to the decision that no keyword research is necessary, when this should never be the case.

I hope that this book has shown that there is a middle ground between these two extremes and good, well researched, keyword data can help you to make better business decisions to help your business both online and offline.

Finding the right keywords, and then ultimately ranking well in the search engines for these terms, can increase the traffic to your website greatly, and by sending high amounts of the right kind of targeted traffic you can increase sales, branding, and develop a strong sustainable business for the future.

The keywords you discover can be used for both PPC and SEO and will ultimately result in a campaign that can send traffic in the short and long term. In addition, the information you discover can help you learn about who your customer is, how they think and what they want.

The online world is constantly changing and updating and it is important that you react alongside it. Through analytics programs and ranking data you can continually monitor the traffic volume coming to you from various keywords, how it is performing and tweak your strategy, website, and budget accordingly. Although keyword research is just one of the steps for a successful online business, it does lay at the foundation of any campaign and it is, therefore, critical that it be performed correctly and thoroughly to give you the best chance for success online.

Online marketing should not be kept in a silo, and the findings you discover from keyword research and analytics should be fed back into the business, and your company data should be used to improve your keyword research. By getting an understanding of your consumers' actions online, what they are looking for and the hot trends, you can design products based around the factors your customers value most and react quickly to their new demands.

You can find the complementary and supplementary products that your customers are searching for, which you don't currently sell. You can also make smarter offline advertising decisions based on growing and declining markets and a better understanding of how to talk to your customer, as their needs are the same whether they are visiting your in person or from behind a screen.

This kind of data can give your business a competitive advantage, to ensure that you, and not your competition, are at the top of Google SERPs when visitors search for your products.

BIBLIOGRAPHY /
ACKNOWLEDGEMENTS /
USEFUL LINKS

Fox, V., 'Marketing in the Age of Google', John Wiley & Sons Inc., New Jersey, 2010

Underhill, P., 'Why We Buy', Simon & Schuster Inc., New York, 2009

Enge, E., Spencer, S., Fichkin, R. and Stricchiola, J.. 'The Art of SEO', O'Reilly Media Inc., Sebastopol, 2010,

Sullivan, D., 'Google Search Share Up After Instant, Yahoo Down After Bing Transition', Search Engine Land, October 2010 *<http://searchengineland.com/google-up-after-instant-yahoo-down-after-bing-52821>*

DeGeyter, S., 'Keyword research and Selection', Pole Position Marketing, *<http://www.polepositionmarketing.com/library/ebooks/keyword-research.pdf>*

The Vertical Measures How-To Guide Series Available Now!

The Vertical Measures How-To Guide Series is for marketers, entrepreneur and executives that are ready to embrace emerging technologies that are taking businesses to the next level. The books highlight tactics that are worth focusing time and effort towards as well as those pointing out pitfalls to avoid.

The series provides deep insights into the world of emerging business technologies and covers topics including; Keyword Research, Facebook, Twitter, Local Search Marketing, Blogging and more.

- Succinct tactics for companies who are either using or plan to use new technologies to grow their business

- Written by industry experts with hands on experience in the field or discipline described

- Written specifically with the business and/or marketing user in mind – combining solid technical expertise with savvy advice.

Get discounted prices and take advantage of the opportunity to receive additional bonus materials for this series and other VM Press books like online at:
www.verticalmeasures.com/store/books

www.ingramcontent.com/pod-product-compliance
Lightning Source LLC
Chambersburg PA
CBHW051238170526
45165CB00004B/1489